THE GREAT BOOK OF
SMALL TALK

Overheard by ANDREW BARROW
Observed by MARC
Introduced by MILES KINGTON

FOURTH ESTATE · LONDON

First published in Great Britain in 1987 by
Fourth Estate Ltd
113 Westbourne Grove
London W2 4UP

Text copyright © 1987 by Andrew Barrow
Illustrations © 1987 by Mark Boxer

British Library Cataloguing in Publication Data

The Great book of small talk.
  1. English wit and humour
  I. Barrow, Andrew
  827'.914'08   PN6175

  ISBN 0-947795-22-7

Typeset in Bembo by MC Typeset Ltd, Chatham, Kent
Printed and bound by The Bath Press, Lower Bristol
Road, Bath BA2 3BL

C O N T E N T S

When I was literary editor of *Punch* in the 1970s, I received a bunch of pieces from Andrew Barrow which were quite unlike any other pieces we got at *Punch*. I had never heard of Andrew Barrow, probably because he had never been published anywhere, but I could recognise a good idea when I saw one. What he had done was to describe a series of episodes in his life using only the words spoken by the people involved.

For instance, one of the pieces was called 'My Life as an Assistant Cinema Manager' and started something like this . . .

> *Manager: Have you been in cinemas before?*
> *Commissionaire: D'take sugar in tea?*
> *Manager: Once you get used to the hours it's alright.*

         . . . and so on, through three weeks at the cinema until Andrew was inevitably fired. I loved these little stories and managed to persuade the editor to print a few of them, thus becoming the first enlightened person to spot an emerging talent. I looked forward to seeing Andrew Barrow put a collection of these pieces together for his first book. This duly came out and it was something else completely different. In fact he has written a small library of books by now and they have all been completely different – collections of gossip, memoirs of odd vicars, charts of relationships between unexpected people among them. But none contained the overheard remarks which I thought was his speciality . . .

The only thing which seems to connect all Andrew Barrow's books is that he is not in them – I mean, he plays the role of the invisible observer – so whenever I have met him subsequently I have urged him to get down those overheard remarks which he did so well for *Punch* and for which he seems to be cut out. Finally he has, and this is it, and this really is the way that people talk. Not all people, but certainly the people near whom Andrew Barrow hovers invisibly, and I think it makes wonderful reading. I wish I'd written it myself.

MILES KINGTON

PARTY TALK

'Is lover boy coming?'

You look bloody fed up

> *People sneer at pink champagne but, my God, it's lovely stuff*

I'm getting deafened in my left ear

> *I'm lucky. I travelled three times round the world before I was twenty-one. I didn't get married till I was thirty-one*

I still think Scorpio men are the most interesting in the world

> *The point is that divorce proceedings are taking so long he might go back to her*

You sound terrible. Have you got a cold?

> *They bunged me into a National Health bed. I was there for three days and then Mama rang up*

Does he still drink an immense amount?

> *Food is such a bore. It always affects me*

By sheer coincidence, two friends of mine have been involved in colossal domestic upheavals this week

> *You really are a terrible old gossip*

New York can be very lonely

Owning a flat can be absolute hell

Any chance of you bailing me out tomorrow? I'm one man short

He's still very immature and needs a lot of corners knocking off

Where are you residing now? World's End? That's a funny old place to live

Somehow I was banking on you being able to help me out on Saturday

He's always doing mad things

I had a typewriting accident. My finger slipped through the keyboard

I really wouldn't recommend experimentation in that quarter

I loved New York

Don't be silly, darling. You hated it

Is lover boy coming?

Look, Bruce, I don't make insulting remarks about your girlfriends

> *She's very omniverous*

Which duchess did he ditch me for?

> *Are you a couple? I hope Howard won't be offended if I don't ask him to dinner*

You see what I mean. Boring beyond belief

> *I'll give a party for you. Let's fix a date now*

You've got a very dirty mind, John

> *That girl is a disaster. Were you here when she fell over and broke everything? What does she do?*

You must have lifted quite a lot of stones to find this lot

> *I'm offering a thousand pounds to anyone who can find me a husband*

I must just go to the loo. Then I'm ready to come with you

> *You were doing your slightly insulting number*

How do you know Reggie?

*What was the name of that chap who used to take
photographs of queers in opium dens in Paris? He
was queer himself, wasn't he?*

I've never known her refuse a party

*He has to sell himself the entire time. If he didn't,
he'd be completely ignored. I tried to mob him up
once and he couldn't take it*

When are you and Susy going to get married?

She had me in stitches

Send her my love, anyway

*It's always you sober-looking fellows who drink a
lot*

She'll be a very late developer. She's exactly like me
at that age. If she really gets stuck into her work,
she could do anything

*The fact that you wake up every morning is
wonderful*

He's afraid I'll go back to my old life and desert him

Bye darling. Thank you. You were a great support

Are you in love with red bottom?

[14]

'A good Sauternes, to me, is absolute heaven'

I smashed down my boyfriend's door with a bag of empty Pimms bottles. He called the police and I haven't seen him since

He's been completely smashed up by the publicity machine

She's not interested in other women

Have another glass of wine, James, and your comprehension will be a bit sharper

Hello, sexy!

I fear he'll never marry. I've had that feeling since he was seventeen

A good Sauternes, to me, is absolute heaven. To me, it's the most gorgeous wine of all

I'm afraid I've got to press on down to Petersfield tonight

I can easily walk home

Tony's thrilled with the carving set. He's a great cook

They've been living on their credit cards. He's now receiving electric shock treatment. They haven't got a bean now

You must let me know whether you're going to
bring John. It's entirely up to you

> *There's a bit of a fug in here*

I hate to say this but I think what you're saying is
utter balls

> *The trouble with William is he's too proud to make
> new friends*

No thanks – oh yes perhaps I will

> *Now what can we do about your love life?*

She's got it made, I should think, gallivanting
around every night of the week

> *You're only young once*

Apparently Roger's given Emma the boot

> *Don't bother. If it's an awful nuisance, don't worry*

Gosh, I envy them. Lucky sods!

> *You haven't seen our wedding
> photographs yet, have you?*

I'm sure I know that woman

D'you want a cigarette, luv?

I think I'll take the proverbial taxi

Hang around!

Apparently he goes off his nut sometimes. Has nervous breakdowns

William has been bitten by the love bug

I'm absolutely livid that my parents are being so petty minded

You missed a marvellous party last night

The bitch didn't invite me

My dear Tim! Bless you!

And then there was that other incident I mentioned

She was being exceptionally stroppy on the telephone

Bats are only flying rats, after all

The thing is I'm literally running from one appointment to another the whole weekend. Also, my mother-in-law's just had a heart attack

Do you know everybody?

> *He's got an inferiority complex on account of his famous dad*

Oh look, Anne's had her hair dyed like an old tart!

> *Certainly as far as I'm concerned, he's one of the best friends I've ever had. He suggested it once and that was it. I have no feelings for him whatsoever other than that I love chatting with him and going out with him*

I'm first and foremost a sporting lass

> *I'm all for Mrs. Jones. She's one of my pals. She really is an A1 sort of person*

I've still got a couple of nasty moves up my sleeve

> *You and I, dear, will be friends for ever*

He means well

> *But does he?*

Hello, precious

> *You are going to have dinner with me. This I do insist*

I bet when you're forty you'll wish you'd married me

> *Until their father drops dead, those girls will all be lost souls*

I hate this sort of party

> *Let's call each other in due course*

Most solicitors I know are unbelievably discreet

> *Mark and Hugo shared a flat in Paris. I was in love with them both*

The family's re-grouping. Serena's just gone to the airport to meet her parents

> *I just find her parties terribly exhausting. By the time you sit down to dinner you're usually so drunk you can't remember who you sat next to*

Not for me, Charles. Last drink for today

> *I don't want any of those people who've got the media at their fingertips*

I'm going home and then I'm going straight out to another party

> *The loo's through there on the left*

'Now what can we do about your love life?'

You're not driving down to Philippa's now, are you? I've got a crate of wine in the back of the car I wanted to give her

> *She seems to have fallen in love with her own press releases*

No writer has a happy sex life

> *I'll be wildly jealous if I see you with another girl*

The nurse said "Shall I ring you if anything happens in the night?"

> *I may be in love with you*

Am I forgiven for last time?

> *That's the most boring remark I've heard all evening*

I know the Sainsbury family relatively well, I might add

> *Would you like a cigarette? I am in a position of being able to offer you one*

D'you want to get rid of us?

> *He's a brilliant businessman and an incredible social climber. He knows exactly who everyone is*

T A L K

I've just been cleaning up someone's flat to give a
party in

Is my mascara running?

I haven't seen you around

I haven't been around

When you try to tease him, he teases you back

*If you've got a screwed up back, hang from the door
lintel and then lie in the sun for half an hour*

Did you hear all that?

*She drinks a terrible lot and behaves very, very
badly*

I've seen her on telly and she's terrifyingly
articulate

All conversations are interesting after a few drinks

He's very devious sexually. He has multiple tastes

She's got no dirty tricks department

Shall we call a truce now?

*We've got a mixture of youngies and oldies
coming on Monday*

'You are going to have dinner with me. This
I do insist'

He really is the most screwed up man I know. I
ended up in a hotel with him at five o'clock in the
morning. He wanted to do all sorts of things. He
was far too sophisticated for me

> *Do you ever sweat like a pig in the middle of the
> night?*

I know what. Your mother should meet my mother

> *You don't have to agree with everything I say. You
> can slap my face if you want*

Have you got a spare hand for a drink?

> *I think we're both on her black list*

I've even got a wheelchair she could occupy

> *Everyone says you've landed on your feet at last*

I was thinking about you in the supermarket

> *My voice was probably rising to a crescendo by this
> time because I was getting pretty pissed*

He's the sort of person you go up to at a party and
they cut you dead

> *He's someone I knew from way back and the funny
> thing is we had just been talking about him*

They now think it's gallstones

Sally's in the big league now

Bear in mind that I'll be out all day

I slept with him once. Oh well about five times. He asked me to marry him – then I suddenly had a revelation about him

I've got absolutely no time for time-wasters

Hello and goodbye!

He's a typical standoffish pansy who obviously hates women

However did you become part of this set?

I'm more solvent now than I've ever been

Could you possibly change the subject?

Jane's gone to the seaside. Under duress

Still got your mini?

I left three messages on her answering machine but now even that's broken down

'*Mark and Hugo shared a flat in Paris. I was
in love with them both*'

John's in hospital with a twisted gut

Oh, Adam, you're depressing me so much!

D'you know that man Bruno? I took two or three looks at him and really, no thank you

I don't like the hostess's brother. Maybe he's nervous or something

Maybe we've come to an emotional full-stop

He's one of my best, best friends

I have an absolute horror of blind dates

She's already broken up three marriages

What he likes doing is doing huge business deals and screwing beautiful girls. Everything else for him is a complete waste of time

She seems to feature at parties now

I couldn't leave Sam even if I wanted to. I just couldn't do it to him

Darling heart, we must leave now

That's his way. You have to quarrel with him all the time or he gets bored

Her scene is galas and balls, not South Bank intellectual

> *I'm having an affair with a lorry driver at the minute*

I've had four major operations and four minor ones

> *Divorce is a bore at the time but it's all for the best in the long run*

What she really likes is just to grumble

> *My car spends more time being fixed and having new wings fitted than actually being driven*

Did you manage to park all right?

> *Sticking together for the sake of the children is a load of bloody nonsense*

Some people seem to have fallen by the wayside

> *Got a fag?*

 Luckily, I had some valium with me

> *What's he like?*

Nice. Obviously. Or I wouldn't like him

I didn't mean that

Everybody goes a bit odd after forty. Married people are just better at covering it up

Are you still in a huff?

I don't want to sleep with you. Or be with you. Period

Don't talk to me about gulls' eggs. I simply loathe them

Hello m'darling!

She says he's no good at all after lights out

I must go to the bathroom

You're lying through the teeth

Does the good woman have any whisky in the house?

I suppose you think it's terribly rude of me to prefer going to a film to human company? It's just that it's a film I've been longing to see for six years

It's depressing because he's not in love with her

I had no idea you had become such a cult figure

[30]

I've got a very bright godson that I'm very fond of who wants to be a doctor

> *Of course you can have a jolly good brain and still be an idiot*

This is rather a dull party, as a matter of fact

> *Goodbye, Rupert. Sweet of you to give us your support*

I had lunch with her last week and she's madder than ever

> *Shove that bottle around, Tony, dear*

Basically I've just fallen completely out of love. I've got nothing whatsoever to say to him now

> *Thank God I'm married*

Last cigarette coming up, luv

> *I think Peter's a bit pissed*

Do you drink more now you're married?

> *No, far less. I used to get really drunk and couldn't remember where I'd been. I loved it*

Such a clean girl, aren't we?

'Am I forgiven for last time?'

Let me give you an ashtray

Your mama is so happy. It's wonderful to see her happy again

You've packed in more experiences than I have. I have fought shy of certain situations

She's only thinking about the carpets

I really think we must start thinking about making a move

I must go and get some sleep

It's amazing. If you know one famous person in London, you know them all. Antony Blond always says hello to me now

I think I will totter

David, you're liable to capsize any moment

Would you excuse me? I must go to the loo

I'm worth tuppence halfpenny

I've had every inch of my face complimented. Even my mole

The only thing is I've promised to drive someone to Devon this weekend who's blind in one eye

I didn't know you could drive

Love is ten times more important than sex

I can hardly keep my eyes open

I usually sleep out, luv

D'you want to top up?

I'll tell you some other time

I've lost my car keys

She's not unintelligent. I believe her cousin's Dean of York. There must be a bit of brain somewhere. Dean of York

I can honestly say I have not enjoyed a single party since I got married

At least he had the graciousness to send a message of apology

I regard you as my greatest friend

I'd quite like to see Sarah again, in a funny sort of way

[34]

The dear old thing dresses rather well, as a matter of fact

> *Well, there's fish pie and fish pie*

I've got a cold coming on so I won't kiss you

> *My first wife kept introducing me to people I had absolutely no rapport with*

He's an ace one sponge

> *He's not interested in women*

I've been so busy going out to din-dins

> *Sal's the worst I've ever come across. She claims to smoke eighty a day*

You branch off before Newmarket, don't you?

> *I shall hang around like a bad fairy at your wedding*

What was I going to say? Something

> *I always go berserk when my mother's here*

Make up your mind, for heaven's sake

*What's the best way from here? By the M4 or
Basingstoke?*

Adrian, your mind is wandering. Have another
drink

*I'm only really frightened of going mad. Having
another nervous breakdown. I've had two very
small nervous breakdowns. More physical than
mental. It's boring. It's horrible. It's not going to
happen again. It won't happen again*

In actual fact, one's parents have no right at all to
butt into one's life

*The important thing in life is being around and
helping people who need help*

Must whizz!

Well, love, call round and see you anon!

I think I'm getting to the stage where you like
younger men

I'm sorry but I'm just not in the mood for Peter

I'm sorry the eats were a bit scruffy by the time you
arrived

James is just chasing his own tail

'She's already broken up three marriages'

You've not got a drink, Nick. What can I get you?

No, Anne, John doesn't hate you. He thought you hated him

So he's fine. Which is nice. Because I was a bit worried about him

She must be a nutcase that girl who married George

I've been walking around in a daze ever since

Where are you residing now?

Beaufort Street

Oh, frightfully grand!

I think the thing is we are all the most tremendous friends

He was one of the most suburban men I've ever met

Are you frightfully pompous now?

Oh, are you going to be lovely and rich?

Mental trouble, is it?

No need to be slightly impertinent

He sat there for five hours and I couldn't get him to say a single sensible thing

> *At this stage I was going out with the most common little man you can imagine. But there were two million reasons for doing so*

She's in love with him and he can't get out of it, poor fellow

> *If Sal didn't enjoy herself, it's her own stupid fault*

What's the problem? Does she drink?

> *I had a telephone call from Caroline this morning. I think we're going to see something of each other next weekend*

Patrick said "What are you doing going around with that bank clerk?"

> *I've just had an idea. A marvellous idea*

I've just had the most hideous thought

> *Ulcers always flare up if you drink. Jeremy Cooper had one*

'Do you know everyone here?'

I was wearing a trouser suit which cost a bomb

She only came off the pill at Christmas

Peter's a sort of semi, semi invalid

I make money stretch fantastically I can tell you

Oh, don't be like that

I think I'll just give Michael a ring in case he's got lumbered with a client

Peter and I talked and talked and talked until five in the morning

Are you a single bird?

Obviously, I'm more than fascinated by you

I came out with so many bon mots on Saturday I can't remember

If I get one original thought, it's treasured. You're going to hear about it for the next ten years

I'm still three-quarters friendly with him

Somebody's pinched my bird

They say whisky depresses you. I tell you it does

'Let me give you an ashtray'

He's a very attractive man but he thinks business
twenty-four hours a day

> *Gulp that down quickly and I'll*
> *get you another*

Lucretia thought you were rather silly

> *I'm off to Paris for two days, I'm happy to say. To*
> *visit our laboratories*

I went out to din–dins every night last week

> *My mother keeps passing out and then being*
> *violently sick*

That was very uncalled for

> *I've had enough of inadequate men*

I wonder why you bother

> *He looks a million years old now*

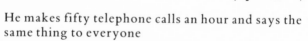

He makes fifty telephone calls an hour and says the
same thing to everyone

> *Sue's mother was in a terrible tizz. She was*
> *beginning to imagine the worst had happened*

Are you always so aggressive?

He seems quite intelligent underneath all that mad exterior

Are you sure it isn't just that she doesn't fancy you?

Nick's a complete baby. He doesn't know what an adult relationship is all about

Let's just say I have a clinical interest in you

Let's have another drink

No, my dear, honestly. I'm perfect. Really I'm fine

Do you still live in Mayfair?

Well I do and I don't

The moment I got into her flat I knew I was home and dry

Why are you smiling in that mad way?

I'm looking forward to it no end

They now think it's a pinched nerve

I don't blame Claire's parents for being suspicious

He's deeply obsequious in a way that's cringingly embarrassing

> *She won't sell that flat in a hurry*

She doesn't eat much but then she never has

> *The little bit of capital I've got, it's virtually gone now anyway*

You seem to be living the life of Riley

> *I'm afraid I can't remember your first name*

I thought it was terribly disappointing. I thought it was just short of disaster

> *As far as I'm concerned, it was a lot better than I thought*

We nearly divorced over it

> *Oh really?*

I'm afraid that woman is the kiss of death on any enterprise

> *I can never think of anything to say to her*

I've had a very close relationship with him ever since. We're not poofs or anything

'At this stage I was going out with the most common little man you can imagine. But there were two million reasons for doing so'

Am I boring you?

What are you sniggering about?

I've got a mouth ulcer. A very bad one

You've gone red

Do you know each other?

Cut to the quick, Andrew. I really am

I'm bored to death too

Sweetie, we must go on our travels

*The awful thing is we must
follow suit*

An awful lot of my friends have died recently

I hear Polly's been burgled. She hasn't told you?

Nobody knows anything about his private life

*Entre nous, Sally said she had supper with him a
fortnight ago and was really most embarrassed and
bored by the whole thing*

I actually have two frying pans because I often cater
for large numbers

It's the strangest thing I've ever heard in my life

He had a boyfriend. Then he had a girlfriend. Then the boyfriend went off with the girlfriend

She's an opportunist. She just wants to go to everything she's invited to

Anne's mini-cab's just arrived

I'd like to see you sometime without your ladies-in-waiting

I was going to ring up and say thanks for a marvellous meal

Bye-bye Paul. Bye-bye Judy

You're coming to dinner on Tuesday. I don't care what you're doing. You'll have to cancel it

Do you know everyone here?

Can I take a note of your number?

Let's not talk about your spectacles

I'm afraid we've got to slip away because we've got baby-sitters and things

Didn't we meet with Jonathan and Lilla?

He's a great fan of yours and is longing to meet you

>*I will, if I may, just give another ring to the AA*

Isn't he ever so slightly gay?

>*Jane's very much on my conscience at the moment*

Yes, the buggers, I was really looking forward to it

>*I've made all my friends now. From now on I'll just make acquaintances*

I'm not a natural games player. I usually make a terrible fool of myself

>*Come and meet a friend of Philip's – you know Philip – who's a sort of journalist. Isn't that right, Adam?*

What a shame you weren't there!

>*Listen, Nigel. Try and make it down to Cookham on Sunday. About eleven o'clock*

I shall be vanishing some time in July. Otherwise I'm around

>*Are you sure it isn't our turn to entertain you?*

Hey, Margie, give us a ring!

'No, my dear, honestly. I'm perfect. Really
I'm fine'

I'm exceedingly well, thank you

Yum! Yum! Yum!

Come to lunch on Friday and I'll poison you

I'll do anything for filthy lucre

Help yourself to a drink

I'm sorry I cut you dead earlier

I didn't notice

One o'clock in the morning, I get some of my best ideas. Get into the office. Type 'em out

Have you got a girlfriend?

I suppose I have in a way. She's been away for the last four months

I think I might just to Corfu next week

D'you think so? You are nice

I tried to tell you earlier in the conversation but you didn't seem to notice

Where can I go and have a pee?

OFFICE TALK

'Trevor doesn't stop at stealing other
people's ideas'

T   A   L   K

This I will do, but sharpish

> *Is it possible to say when she would be available?*

I just get out of the Underground, stagger a
hundred yards and I'm here

> *It's a waste of blood time*

Initial signals I get from him tell me he's rather a
good man

> *Could I be very rude and take a cigarette? I'm
> absolutely dying*

I've got so much work to do it's ridiculous

> *Job prospects aren't frightfully hot, I'm afraid*

I've heard funny reports about him. Apparently he
always brings someone with him called John

> *Come in. Squat down*

Trevor doesn't stop at stealing other people's ideas

> *I've got quite a perceptive little brain box you
> know*

One of these days we must fix a meeting where I can
buy you lunch afterwards

I believe he's having quite a relaxed sort of day today, as a matter of fact

She's got the whole thing buggered up actually but who am I to say it?

Not in yet. Judging by the non-presence of his coat

I haven't heard much yet but apparently they weren't exactly jumping about with joy

Hello George!

Christ, come in!

That wildly efficient secretary makes me feel slightly agitated

Keep quiet with the patter and exude confidence

Yes indeed. What about lunch?

Could I have a chat with you, Max, for about five minutes?

Now you know why I gave up chemistry at school

It's a point of view. Not one on which I'd take issue

8.30 in the morning? I shall be speaking to him severely, with rage

Tickle him under the chin if he gets obstreperous!

He's still on the phone. He won't be a sec

Hello, could I speak to – Christ, I've forgotten his name!

I got the brush off in a big way

Hi, Nobby, congratulations! Well deserved if I may say so

Is this tea or coffee?

Hugh's on the phone at this precise moment

He's the biggest load of wet flab I've ever come across

No, the person you want to speak to is on holiday

They've upped the quantity and the other thing is they want it in a screaming hurry

What John was doing was, quite obviously, stalling

Of course he's trying to replace Phil Martin

Which I think is a dirty one

Oh I think Phil can look after himself

O F F I C E

Her usual Monday morning sickness. She must have
wild weekends

> *D'you want my elegantly styled boot in your groin?*

I'm not going to divulge any more to you

> *I'm sure there's something nice underneath but I
> can't get through to it*

I've given it up, my dear. I haven't smoked for a
fortnight

> *She's moaning like mad at the moment because we
> haven't got a car*

Seems feasible to me

> *Some of the things I know about this place would
> astound you*

What's today? Tuesday or Wednesday?

> *Tuesday*

It feels like fucking Thursday!

> *Is he a drag or is he nice?*

This is the sort of morning people commit suicide

Well, I've already done so

You won't let him get away without phoning me, will you?

There's a distinct lack of oxygen in this place

Can I cadge a fag off you?

You didn't come to Vicky's farewell

I wasn't asked

My wife drove me to Hadley Wood Station. It was locked to my consternation. We had to drive to Cockfosters

I've got three meetings on Wednesday morning

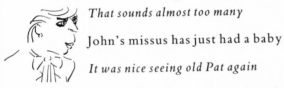

That sounds almost too many

John's missus has just had a baby

It was nice seeing old Pat again

It's a bloody bore having a commissionaire who doesn't know people's names

Look out, here's Ernest. You're in Ernest's chair

Old Bertie's quite good in that respect

[59]

John, may I call you John?

I'm just fed up with this afternoon

We had the usual chit-chat

It's just a question of what's cooking. We'll just have to see if it fructifies

Women are all the same

Get off me, you raving homosexual!

Mr. Goodyear sends his apologies. He'll be another couple of minutes

Say hello to Peter for me

I spend half my time answering bloody invoices

This only happens in bloody fairy stories!

Things are moving on this Stevenage thing

He must be prepared to pay me a professional fee. Otherwise I'd just be doing him a favour

Will you give me a tinkle tomorrow morning?

I'd better say goodbye as Hugh was having words with me when the phone rang

'Could I have a chat with you, Max, for about five minutes'

I've just solved a pretty nutty problem

Pay day tomorrow, that's nice

I know more about this than I'm prepared to say

I'm exceedingly unenthusiastic about the whole idea

He went out for a packet of cigarettes and was never heard of again. I often feel like doing it myself

Take your finger out of the palm of my hand, you sexy bastard!

I'm not too keen on your taking personal calls here

Looks as if you're in time for a cup of coffee

You always get beaten down eventually in this place

Are you taking the afternoon off?

I'll see you anon

I want to get out of this business

I'll tell you who lives near you. Sue Hamble

With the proviso that they don't offload their muck
onto me

This firm works on coffee like cars work on petrol

Trevor, get ready to leave at a moment's notice

I'm afraid she's not back from lunch yet

My holiday arrangements are still a bit fluid

*I'm a bit muddled after a
muddling weekend*

I don't know what's worse here.
The tea or the coffee

Look, Sue – it is Sue isn't it?

He's not taking any calls. He'll get the message but
I don't guarantee he'll ring you back

I'll fly and get some coffee!

Where is John? He promised me faithfully he'd be
here at half past three

*Very handsome that. A bit warm
for today I should think*

I'm a bit dozy today. A bit dozier than usual

'Mr Goodyear sends his apologies. He'll be another couple of minutes'

I'm just going to get a hot drink

Sorry, who did you say you were?

John sees Peter as a potential ally

Right, boys and girls, I'm off to lunch

I'm working on one cylinder today

Don't walk away, Brian, while I'm talking to you

Sorry I'm late. I got some cotton wool stuck in my nose and had to pop along to the doctor

Don't let me down this time or I'll throw another tantrum

I smell dirty business

Actually I know for a fact there's some hanky panky going on in Clifford's office

I haven't woken up yet

Someone's head's going to roll

I've got a frantic headache. I think I'll blow off for a bit and lie down

Clifford is clever, in the most evil and scheming way

> *He made me promise not to tell anyone he has
> trouble with the ladies*

It's pouring with rain out there. I can hear it

> *It can rain its blooming head off. It doesn't affect
> us. Unless it's lunch time or going home time*

Cheers. Have a nice weekend!

> *David's mother just died. In the hairdressers*

They've chopped off quite a few people recently

> *I might end up a record holder. Longest
> cold ever*

I'm going to get me a bullet-proof jacket

> *Jesus bloody Christ! What's the matter with them?
> The number's permanently engaged*

Pat and Len, I'm sure I can rely on you to keep this
meeting running briskly

> *I hope there's something good on TV tonight*

Excuse me literally one second. Sorry about that

> *Okeydoke*

'I smell dirty business'

One thing about this place. They've always got tea on tap

Shit! That's my other telephone ringing

No, he doesn't work in this office at all now. He's out on the road. No, I don't know where he is

I shall have a quiet word with Brian Butler. They've even produced a bloody booklet about it. In fact, what I'll do is contact Jimmy Jones

You're busy. I can tell

Begin again. Slowly

I'm slightly pushed this afternoon. I suppose I could grind something out

I explained it all at the bloody time

I thought you were on holiday

Well, I am really

Nothing too finished, you understand

I'm only telling you this because you're a friend

Yes quite

I'll have a natter with Denis on Monday morning

Is that an order, sir?

Kind of very presto indeed

I had fried chicken for lunch and splashed my jacket
a bit

*You know what he's like though. As slippery as a
bloody orange pip*

My nine o'clock meeting never happened which
made me extremely pleased

Hello, Brian, what are you up to?

I'm just dashing off to Milan, that's all

*Given all that and I wouldn't disagree with you for
a moment . . .*

That was disposed of pretty quickly

 *I laughed like a drain when I got your
reply. Great man!*

Your message being what? Sorry

My breakfast takes two minutes flat

'Someone's head is going to roll . . .'

Quite honestly I think she's in no fit state to work at all

If only you knew how bored I am

I think you'd better try to get to the next meeting

She's too adult and she'll have to pay for it

The only thing is I'm off to the States for a couple of weeks

What does he do besides slopping beer back?

Just a moment I'll get a pad

Marvellous, isn't it? I said "Could I speak to Mr. Uke?" and they said "No you can't. He died last night."

I bank at Barclays in the – Christ where is it?

He's in a meeting. As he usually is

Well get him out of there!

I was recounting this story to him without realising who he was

I sometimes wonder if there is such a thing as an interesting job

*Will you hold on for a moment while
I grab a match?*

I must dash

*You've got a meeting with me, John and
Len Webb at ten o'clock*

She hasn't gone very far – judging by the presence
of her spectacles

Don't mention the wife, because she's just died

It's a bit risky, isn't it? If you get any more, you
have to have them kicking around the office floor
and that's where the trouble starts

I've just got to go and have a 'flu shot

On Friday? Oh, *Friday!* Of course, sorry, it didn't
click

*The thing is you get so angry with her and then she
comes round and you feel sorry for her*

If I hear anything I'll call you. Thanks a lot, bye!

Ghost from the past! Nice to see you, Pat

I can't eat in the mornings

'Quite honestly I think she's in no fit state
to work at all'

'Ghost from the past! Nice, to see you, Pat'

*I've only got to poke my nose out of the office and
everybody wants me*

Words literally fail me with you

Mark, can I have a little word with you?

That's your bloody problem

*In retrospect that might have been quite a good
move, actually*

She'll be with you in no time. She's just finishing
something off

Got ten minutes, Andrew?

Sorry to keep you waiting. I had a long tramp

Would you like a cup of machine coffee?

Don't worry about that. It's horse-shit

With what purpose in mind, Andrew?

I've already contracted to go to a meeting at four
o'clock

Yes, it's a gorgeous piece of marketing

My telephone's quiet at the moment

He's in and out today. He's flying up to Newcastle at 7.15 tomorrow morning but he's got to be back by three in the afternoon

If you ring again in five minutes she should be in her office

Hold the line please. Another one of your birds, John

You'll get a decision by the middle of next week

Look some people are just coming into my office for a meeting, so may I ring off?

I should think you might do it rather efficiently

He's just gone out of the room this second. Can I give him a message?

What I'm going to say is nothing, because I'm afraid it's going to have to be a surprise

No, I can't transfer you to Trevor Smith. He's on holiday

It didn't help when Leslie came in. Dying for a chat

Underneath the noise, could I say that you've got a new desk coming next week?

'Yes, it's a gorgeous piece of marketing'

That would be munificence unleashed

> *In the twelve years I've worked in this firm some things have happened which are so nasty you wouldn't believe them*

He's rather difficult to get in touch with. He flits about quite a lot

> *Nineteen minutes to opening time!*

Brian, can you answer that? It's Lorna Winstanley

> *Bless you. You've got me on to a train of thought*

He's happy. He's got a date tonight

> *It all sounds a bit dodgy to me*

I've just had a nasty thought

PUB TALK

*'I don't trust the man. For a start
he doesn't drink'*

You can tell this drink's beginning to work because
I'm beginning to say things I mean

> *Annie was being extremely flirtatious with me last
> night*

He's mad keen to get a new car next year

> *I really ought to say no*

She must have been pissed out of her mind

> *She's got a boyfriend. I've got a girlfriend. We all
> like sex, do me a favour*

She went out to deliver some leaflets and fell down a
man-hole. D'you know what that is? That's love.
Not looking where you're going

> *There are certain subjects which I don't discuss, as
> you well know*

So where have you been? You say you've been
flirting round all over the place?

> *London has got jobs, hasn't it. That's the one
> advantage of it, isn't it?*

There's only one man who's any good at all and
that's David Owen

Could I have ten Piccadilly while you're passing?

Listen, I'm starving and I've got the wherewithal at home to make an enormous salad

I think I'll have an early night

I'm getting deeper and deeper into a mess

Where did you pick up your philosophy of life from? Yourself?

We've chosen rather a draughty place to sit

It's enough to put you off sex. For an hour

Push the door shut, will you, kid? Push the – thanks

All I say is be bloody careful

I had a row with this woman in the park. She said did I believe in Jesus Christ. I said "Well, no, I don't". She said "Why not?" I said "Well look at the facts"

A little bit of John goes a long way

It is a free world. You can do whatever you like and I have no right to object

Of course the other way to make money is to marry a rich lady

D'you remember Jean and Gordon Stacey?

I never met them but I remember them

Well they went on the same trip for eighty-eight quid. Mind you the hotel accommodation was only bed and breakfast

He calls himself a Marxist, the silly fool

Don't be silly. I'm a woman of the world. You can have your own key.

Can I say one thing? Will you shut up a moment?

She studied ballet for seven years. And then had a bad fall. A jump went wrong and she broke both her legs

I saw Peter. He's in a bit of a state, isn't he? He needs a lady

I'm not ill and for God's sake don't call me darling

Come on, Arthur, forget it. For God's sake

Does she take the pill, lad?

> *That's the one thing I don't know. Whether she's bed-conducive or not*

I don't trust the man. For a start he doesn't drink

> *I'm an intellectual. I was at university. All right, I was asked to leave*

Don't call me love. I object to it. I've objected to it for a long time. Why don't you treat me like a lady instead of some cheap little wench?

> *Is it the same guvnor here, Gordon?*

I was in Barnes the other day and I dropped in at the Cricketers for a sandwich – and they've gutted it!

> *We've only got five pubs in Wimblèdon itself – the lower town – and the prices are amazing*

Was there an elderly white-haired man sitting here a minute ago?

> *I don't like to see you without a smoke*

I'll see you later, Curly

> *Are you residing locally?*

There's not one decent pub left in Chelsea

> *Life today is a very tortuous business. Emotionally one tends to take the crunch. I really think the youngsters of today, they are up a gum tree*

I'll pay for these and you can give me a cigarette

> *You're drunk, woman*

There's no complete answer in life. You just have to go along with things

> *It's been cough, cough, cough for the last three weeks and the funny thing is there's been nothing to bring up*

Now he's gone, let's have a chat

> *Hello, who's whipped my bloody beer?*

Apparently she fell out of a taxi when she was pissed

> *Pretty damn funny!*

So what happened to the girl you were living with? What's happened to the girl that was living with you? What's happened to you? Why are you on your own?

Any pies left?

Only sausages

I'd like to get fixed up tonight or tomorrow. Single room with kitchen

I'd like a glass with a little piece of lemon in it, some tonic, some Gordon's and some ice

You're as strong as I am. You're a survivor, I'm a survivor

Finish my drink. It's good but I can't drink that much

It's the cheapest place. Room plus breakfast twelve pounds fifty

We each have our own room, right?

I'll see you later, John. Will you be here later on?

Which part of Ireland do you come from, if you don't mind me asking?

Best of luck, old chap. Nice to meet you

I come from a backwater called Torquay. A *real* backwater

'Like a fool I said "Yes". Then I had to ring back
and say "No"'

I said to her "If the Inland Revenue got onto you, you'd be in Holloway for thirty years"

A pint, you said?

I was accosted by a queer on the Metro in Paris. He wanted to feel my bottom

You're going back to Phoebe. I know your wicked mind. I'll give you a hundred pounds to stay away from the bitch

Are you having it off with that ginger bird?

A brandy, Albert, please

Did you hear what he said? Good job you didn't because it was very rude. He's terrible

I want a proper bed-sittingroom with a telephone in the hall

I've got to the point where I'm so bored of sex anyway. I mean six times a night is nothing for her

How are you doing? All right? Married yet? No? Sensible chap!

*She boozes, I can tell you. She pitches for very
expensive drinks*

You want someone to be really rude to you, don't
you? Why do you provoke?

I like the blighter and I intend to make it obvious

I don't usually speak like this. I've got a funny
throat

*That shepherd's pie is looking rather tired now but
at lunch time it is excellent*

My mother is totally dependent on me

*My father is dying. Dying. He'll be dead in a few
years. I give him three years at the most. I knew he
was dying when I left home*

So many people want me, darling, seriously

*He looks like an old fuddy-duddy
but in fact he's very, very nice*

She was on television again last night.
Ten years ago she was nothing

I'm afraid I'm a bit short of loot

My ex-husband hasn't given me a birthday present

> *They call me George, as if I were an old pal. What
> a nonsense*

My dear girl, the greatest thing in life is friends

> *Don't involve me, darling, for Christ's sake*

I cannot stay in that house any longer because the
atmosphere is so ghastly

> *John, I hate to remind you but
> we've got a train to catch*

I've known real love and you want
to be together the entire time

> *I saw you as a left winger. Lots of clever side-steps*

I'm just going to have a little tidy-uppy

> *Three scotch eggs? D'you want them on separate
> plates?*

I can't bear people who lie in bed all day

> *I'm in a – what's the word – limbo at the moment
> but it's all going to work all right I think*

I watched it on television the other night. I was sitting there sobbing my heart out

> *Hello, babe, where have you been? I've been trying to ring you for three hours*

If I had a chance I'd be wildly pissed now

> *You know who I saw today? Your ex-girlfriend. I'm joking now. You know, the chatterbox. She was having her hair coloured in Irene's*

Terry's got problems. This girl is insisting that he marries her

> *That man has no interests whatsoever. Except sexual*

Why does this idiot have to sit here?

> *Like a fool I said "Yes". Then I had to ring back and say "No"*

God is good. He always gives you a little bit of something to go on

> *I've got all me important things, like me pill*

I'm sorry. It' not all right. I'm pregnant

You don't hit a woman when she's drunk. That's one thing you don't do

There are lots of blokes about like that, aren't there?

She was a bit drunk, mind you

You have to come to Bristol on the twenty-eighth and see me make a fool of myself. Powerboat racing

She's forty odd but has a mental age of one-and-a-half

They're ex-directory and have been for years

Ronnie Barker must be worth a bomb now

Geoff, you're surrounded by women! What's Geoff got that the rest of us haven't?

Don't flinch all the time I'm talking to you

I'm not down on homosexuals but they can be a bloody nuisance

Did I tell you what I was writing my thesis on? The French Matrimonial Property Act

Oh God, you must be out of your tiny mind!

It's the drinking she does at home *that's the trouble*

Three pints of Tartan please. Do you take credit cards?

It's warm in here. It's terribly cold outside. I said to Betty I wish I'd put a cardigan on

I like your speaking voice

You're Jewish, aren't you? Great people the Jews. My great-grandmother was Jewish

Women get old, don't they, and careworn?

I couldn't understand half of what he was saying. I wasn't listening half the time. Was that rude?

Aren't you too hot in that jumper, Jimmy?

D'you know something? I hate to tell you this. I don't agree with you at all

Journalists are very interesting until you get to know them

Life doesn't fall into your lap like that

Thank you sir. You're a gentleman and a scholar

*'Thank you sir, You're a gentleman
and a scholar'*

I'm not interested in helping lame ducks. They can go away and work out their own problems and not inflict them on me

Give me half of Guinness, please darling

I have the evil distinction of being known everywhere

What's he like? Is he nice? Makes you feel at ease?

Is it possible to move your feet just a tiny bit?

I simply cannot understand that muddled woman's mind

She gets away with blue murder that girl. I said "How dare you tell me what to do!"

You're still a man of leisure then? How do you manage it?

For that very unfortunate remark you can buy me an enormous drink

He eventually got the message that I wasn't interested

I'd rather listen to this than screaming bloody pop music all the time

I never drink on my own. That's one thing I don't do. I think that's awfully sad

> *One day I might tell you the story of my life. I won't start now because by the time I'd finished we'd all be too old to care*

Lloyd George was a lecher. He had birds galore

> *OK, so one's vaguely available*

The moment I get my new flat I'm going to lock my door and not drink one drink for a whole week

> *I must go to the gents*

I pass your doorbell sometimes and wonder if I should ring it

> *A pint of bitter, please, Tim*

Do you understand what I'm trying to say to you?

> *She was a woman of about forty, forty-five. She was show business or had been. Anyway she gave me a smacking great kiss*

I feel like death warmed up

> *Lovely pork. Pork with crackling. I love it*

I like leg of lamb. You dip your bread in the juice.
Beautiful!

> *Incidentally would you like to come back and have
> a drink chez moi?*

I want to get married, you see

> *Excuse me, but your bag's digging into my hip bone*

Going back to Torquay is impossible now. Not
because of the peace and quiet – because I love peace
and quiet – but because I can't communicate with
the people. I started to tell you this a moment ago

> *He's been my constant mate through life. This
> week he's on holiday*

D'you think there's going to be a third world war?

> *I do*

I had the nicest bit of fish last night since I've been
in London

> *He's going to win the pools next week, he's assured
> me that. If he wins half a million, we can have a
> couple of drinks on him*

If I married you, I would destroy your life

It's not much take-home pay is it?

He's one of the most genuine people I've ever met. I just find him incredibly easy to talk to

I'll thump you one in a moment. I'll come round and give you one on the ear-hole

What are you smoking that stupid cigar for?

The whole idea of life is just dreadful. You're forever being thrown into the position where you depend upon one person

She was the grand dame of a duke and all that. Very county

I don't indulge in sex for sex's sake

I've got almost a quid to last me until the end of the week

Aaagh! You nearly sent my specs flying!

Bookmakers have got to live, haven't they?

I pay my way through life. Why shouldn't you

I'll see you anon, ladies and gentlemen

'For that very unfortunate remark you can buy
me the most enormous drink'

Loch Ness is mighty deep. There could be two or three monsters down there

She tells me she's still nuts about him

Mind how you go, Stan!

I'll give you my office number. I don't give my home number to anyone. I'm not stupid

I think it's going to be a heavy night on the Carlsberg Specials

I'm told the cocktail's back again

Listen, have you rung Christine?

She said "Hello Pete" and then talked for ages. I couldn't think what to say becasue I didn't know who I was talking to

I've never been a bore in all my life

There's this bird that's very nice. Judy, she's called. She looks ancient but she's very nice

Moving up to North London, are you? You'll be near me

Listen, Fred. Give me back that fiver I gave you

*I'm just cogitating at the moment. I'm certainly not
going to set the world on fire in the next few weeks*

Come on darling, for fuck's sake. Wake up!

*I bought this really to wear in the winter, perhaps
on a sunny sort of day*

He treats his women-folk badly. He had four chicks
up the spout at the same time

*I like genuine sorrow. Not
synthetic sorrow*

Me? Well it all depends

*I love it when unexpected
things happen*

I'm living on yoghurt and yeast
at the moment

*It's not just the day-to-day living. It's things like
water rates for a hundred quid. I mean, how are you
meant to pay that?*

Alan, I'm not awfully certain that I like you

I had this stupid letter from my sister this morning

I was aghast this morning. I had to take the car in for a service and my toes were nearly frozen off as I waited for a taxi

The door slammed on me and took the top of my finger off

I can't get on with my life when you're around

I'm going to get bitchy in a moment. Any moment now I'm going to be bad-tempered

These bloody women are wearing me out

What her old man's worried about is fags on the carpet

If he can't bring out the best in a woman, he's not much of a man

I left my umbrella in the Turk's Head yesterday and I'm terribly unhappy about it

What does your dad say about your shacking up with Mr. Sneedham?

He doesn't say anything

Well he's jolly broad-minded then

Honestly, I don't know why I'm a friend of yours

My father was seriously mentally ill last year but all is well now

Are you as nutty as ever?

Don't look so sad. Have a drink

You're told all about these people, that they're really big, interesting people but they turn out to be dead ordinary

I counted methodically. Like a bloody computer

Hey Fred, when you take a girl out, do you talk Physics all the time?

I want to study drama. I want to be rich. I don't want to go to college any more

Mitchell, Warren, is still very funny

I've met her once. What more do I have to say?

I'm your lower-middle-class stool pigeon

Tony always says "Darling, you look marvellous" when I know bloody well I don't

'*Excuse me, but your bag's digging into my hip bone*'

Look, Frank, listen carefully to what I'm going to say

She works her arse off fourteen hours a day

If you can afford to pay the gas and electricity then you're laughing

I thought, Christ, do I look that old?

She's a little devil. She really is

D'you want to go and freshen up?

Tina never sounds very satisfied, does she? I don't think she likes getting older. I think she still wants to be flitting around with men

Bloody hell. That was quick

Who's this latest man? You've teased me now

He's at clergy college

So he bums off again. It's really weird the way he does that. No one even knows his name. Dick or Mick or something

You can't help seeing the funny side of it

You are a bloody liar

I am not a bloody liar

I've got a brother who soaks everything in sauce

They were playing Bob Dylan till four in the morning. I could hear every single bloody word. So I called the police

I'm not a superman, Alex. Any more than you are

This was – oh Christ – twenty-four years ago now

In the meantime, what if she finds out about me?

Hello, mate. How are you?

My mum and dad are splitting up

I can't stand flies. I'd sooner have a beetle than fly. They get up to all sorts of things, flies

I crept back to town at about ten o'clock

That guy gives me the shits

Have you met his girlfriend, his live-in lady?

I seem to be having such rotten luck lately

> *We all have skeletons in the cupboard, if that's
> what you mean*

He was getting a bit shirty at one moment

> *I thought Mr. Richards was a bit of a villain*

He is. Was and is. But it isn't always easy to get rid
of a person like that

> *That was the night Spurs walloped Chelsea
> seven one*

What you want to do is get married. You'd make a
marvellous father. Have children. Why not?

> *While you've been away, Jean has made two calls
> to Australia*

I want to die

> *You may think it but you mustn't say it, Betty*

Why not? It's true. I want to die

> *If my memory serves me right, I don't think I've
> ever known it so cold*

Are you going up by train?

> *No, coach*

Coach? Jolly good!

> *Oh my goodness I'm not sitting there. He's literally spewed all down himself*

She's late today. I suppose he's kept her busy

> *She's only about fifty but she's already had her face lifted four times*

Bloody next night, I saw her in The Queen's Head

> *I like Bob Dylan but not for four solid hours in the middle of the night*

She has relations. A niece

> *Terrible cut throat mob down there, Bill*

I'll tell you what. I'll have half of Guinness

> *I gave Joe a bed for the night and he slept terribly badly*

Who the hell is she? Or is she nobody?

'*What does your dad say about you shacking
up with Mr Sneedham?*'

*I had a Japanese friend. God I'd like to see him
again. He was called Kiwi*

She is a woman who pretends to know everything
about every subject

Sam fell for me in a very big way

I have no intention of staying sober this evening.
I'm not going to get very pissed

What's the news on your mortgage?

Anne, did you enjoy being with Tim or did he make
a neurotic wreck of you?

*Could you – would you mind moving that chair
just a tiny bit for someone who's crippled
to get through?*

He hasn't got a tremendous lot of self-confidence

*He's not terribly attractive and I think was feeling
a bit randy*

My father was a super man. There's no doubt about
that. But he married the greatest bitch of all time

What's his flat like? Is it nice?

Never seen it. Never been invited

**'They were playing Bob Dylan till four
in the morning'**

I haven't eaten since last night

Will you marry me? Oh it's too late? You've just got married?

He really is the most boring man I know

Hello, someone's on the red biddy

I'm in love. Not Sue. Another Sue. It's a very uptight situation

Sex is hell when you're pissed, it really is

We've all been to hell and back

There's nothing in this world I'd like more at the moment than a pee